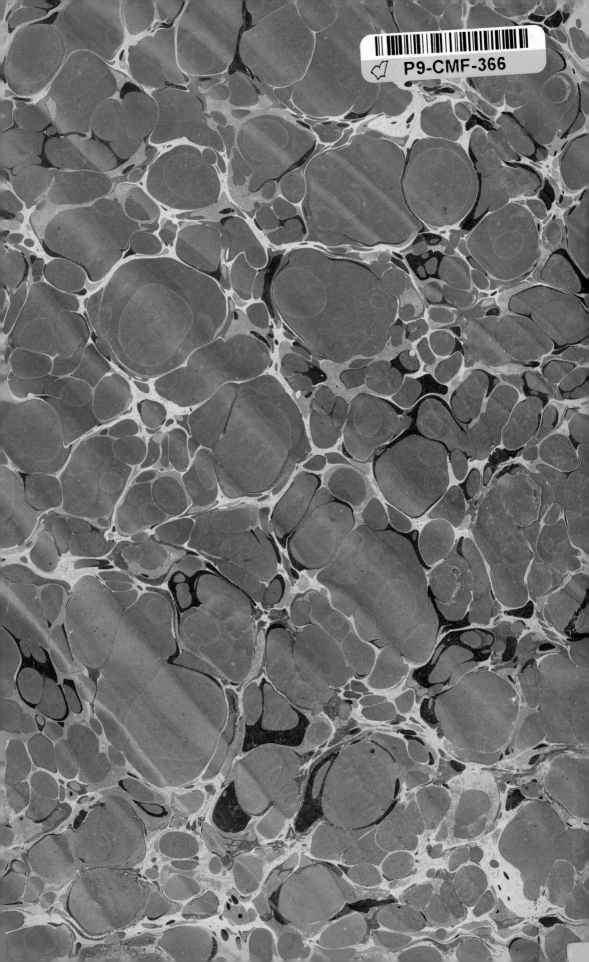

3516
4
#5 - 2 vols

GUIZOT'S GIBBON.

HISTORY

OF

THE DECLINE AND FALL

OF THE

ROMAN EMPIRE.

BY EDWARD GIBBON, ESQ.

A NEW EDITION REVISED AND CORRECTED THROUGHOUT, PRECEDED BY A PREFACE, AND ACCOMPA-
NIED BY NOTES, CRITICAL AND HISTORICAL, RELATING PRINCIPALLY
TO THE PROPAGATION OF CHRISTIANITY:

BY M. F. GUIZOT,

MINISTER OF PUBLIC INSTRUCTION FOR THE KINGDOM OF FRANCE.

THE PREFACE, NOTES AND CORRECTIONS, TRANSLATED FROM THE FRENCH EXPRESSLY FOR THIS EDITION.

WITH

A NOTICE OF THE LIFE AND CHARACTER OF GIBBON,

AND

WATSON'S REPLY TO GIBBON.

IN TWO VOLUMES.
VOL. 1.

CINCINNATI:
J. A. & U. P. JAMES, WALNUT STREET,
BETWEEN FOURTH AND FIFTH.
1850.

CONTENTS.

VOL. I.

CHAPTER I.

The extent and military force of the empire, in the age of the Antonines.

A. D.		Page
	INTRODUCTION. Moderation of Augustus. Imitated by his successors	13
	Conquest of Britain was the first exception to it. Conquest of Dacia, the second exception to it. Conquests of Trajan in the east	14
	Resigned by his successor Hadrian. Contrast of Hadrian and Antoninus Pius. Pacific system of Hadrian and the two Antonines. Defensive wars of Marcus Antoninus. Military establishment of the Roman emperors	15
	Discipline. Exercises. The legions under the emperors	16
	Arms. Cavalry. Auxiliaries	17
	Artillery. Encampment. March. Number and disposition of the legions. Navy	18
	Amount of the whole establishment. View of the provinces of the Roman empire. Spain. Gaul. Britain. Italy	19
	The Danube and Illyrian frontier. Rhætia, Noricum and Pannonia. Dalmatia. Mæsia & Dacia. Thrace. Macedonia and Greece. Asia Minor.	20
	Syria. Phœnicia and Palestine	21
	Egypt. Africa. The Mediterranean with its islands	22
	General idea of the Roman empire	

CHAPTER II.

Of the union and internal prosperity of the Roman empire in the age of the Antonines.

	Principles of government. Universal spirit of toleration. Of the people. Of philosophers	22
	Of the magistrates. In the provinces. At Rome. Freedom of Rome	23
	Italy. The provinces. Colonies and municipal towns	24
	Division of the Latin and the Greek provinces. General use of both the Greek and Latin languages. Slaves	25
	Their treatment. Enfranchisement	26
	Numbers. Populousness of the Roman empire. Obedience and union. Roman monuments. Many of them erected at private expense	27
	Example of Herodes Atticus. His reputation. Most of the Roman monuments for public use. Temples, theatres, aqueducts	28
	Number and greatness of the cities of the empire. In Italy. Gaul and Spain. Africa. Asia	29
	Roman roads. Posts. Navigation. Improvement of agriculture in the western countries of the empire. Introduction of fruits, &c. The vine. The olive	30
	Flax. Artificial grass. General plenty. Arts of luxury. Foreign trade. Gold and silver. General felicity	31
	Decline of courage. Of genius. Degeneracy	32

CHAPTER III.

Of the constitution of the Roman empire, in the age of the Antonines.

	Idea of a monarchy. Situation of Augustus	32
	He reforms the senate. Resigns his usurped power. Is prevailed upon to resume it under the title of emperor, or general. Power of the Roman generals	33
	Lieutenants of the emperor. Division of the provinces between the emperor and the senate. The former preserves his military command, and guards, in Rome itself. Consular and tribunitian powers	34
	Imperial prerogatives. The magistrates. The senate. General idea of the imperial system	35
	C.urt of the emperors. Deification. Titles of *Augustus* and *Cæsar*. Character and policy of Augustus	36
	Image of liberty for the people. Attempts of the senate after the death of Caligula. Image of government for the armies. Their obedience. Designation of a successor. Of Tiberius. Of Titus	37

A. D.		Page
96	The race of the Cæsars, and Flavian family. Adoption and character of	
116	Trajan. Of Hadrian. Adoption of the elder and younger Verus. Adop-	
138—180	tion of the two Antonines	38
	Character and reign of Pius. Of Marcus. Happiness of the Romans. Its precarious nature. Memory of Tiberius, Caligula, Nero, and Domitian. Peculiar misery of the Romans under their tyrants	39
	Insensibility of the Orientals. Knowledge and free spirit of the Romans. Extent of their empire left them no place of refuge	40

CHAPTER IV.

The cruelty, follies, and murder of Commodus. —Election of Pertinax.—His attempts to reform the state.—His assassination by the prætorian guards.

	Indulgence of Marcus	40
180	To his wife Faustina. To his son Commodus. Accession of the emperor Commodus. Character of Commodus. His return to Rome.	41
183	Is wounded by an assassin. Hatred and cruelty of Commodus towards the senate. The Quintilian brothers.	
186	The minister Perennius. Revolt of Maternus	42
189	The minister Cleander. His avarice and cruelty. Sedition and death of Cleander. Dissolute pleasures of Commodus	43
	His ignorance and low sports. Hunting of wild beasts. Commodus displays his skill in the amphitheatre. Acts as a gladiator. His infamy and extravagance	44
192	Conspiracy of his domestics. Death of Commodus. Choice of Pertinax for emperor. He is acknowledged by the prætorian guards. And by the	
193	senate. The memory of Commodus declared infamous	45
	Legal jurisdiction of the senate over the emperors. Virtues of Pertinax. He endeavours to reform the state. His regulations. His popularity	46
	Discontent of the prætorians. A conspiracy prevented. Murder of Per-	
193	tinax by the prætorians	47

CHAPTER V.

Public sale of the empire to Didius Julianus by the prætorian guards. — Clodius Albinus in Britain, Pescennius Niger, in Syria, and Septimius Severus, in Pannonia, declare against the murderers of Pertinax.—Civil wars and victory of Severus over his three rivals.—Relaxation of discipline.—New maxims of government.

	Proportion of the military force to the number of the people. The institution of the prætorian guards. Their camp, strength, and confidence	47
193	Their specious claims. They offer the empire to sale. It is purchased by Julian. Julian is acknowledged by the senate. Takes possession of the palace	48
	The public discontent. The armies of Britain, Syria, and Pannonia, declare against Julian. Clodius Albinus in Britain. Pescennius Niger in Syria	49
193	Pannonia and Dalmatia, Septimius Severus. Declared emperor by the Pannonian legions. Marches into Italy. Advances towards Rome. Distress of Julian. His uncertain conduct	50
	Is deserted by the prætorians. Is condemned and executed by order of the senate. Disgrace of the prætorian guards. Funeral and apotheosis of	
193—197	Pertinax. Success of Severus against Niger and against Albinus. Conduct of the two civil wars. Arts of Severus. Towards Niger	51
	Towards Albinus. Event of the civil wars. Decided by one or two battles. Siege of Byzantium	52
	Death of Niger and Albinus. Cruel consequences of the civil wars. Animosity of Severus against the senate. The wisdom and justice of his government. General peace and	

A. D.		Page
	prosperity. Relaxation of military discipline	53
	New establishment of the prætorian guards. The office of prætorian præfect. The senate oppressed by military despotism. New maxims of the imperial prerogative	54

CHAPTER VI.

The death of Severus.—Tyranny of Caracalla. —Usurpation of Macrinus.—Follies of Elagabalus.—Virtues of Alexander Severus.—Licentiousness of the army.—General state of the Roman finances.

	Greatness and discontent of Severus. His wife the empress Julia. Their two sons, Caracalla and Geta. Their mutual aversion to each other	
208	Three emperors. The Caledonian war. Fingal and his heroes	55
211	Contrast of the Caledonians and Romans. Ambition of Caracalla. Death of Severus, and accession of his two sons. Jealousy and hatred of the two emperors. Fruitless negociation for dividing the empire between them.	
212	Murder of Geta	56
213	Remorse and cruelty of Caracalla. Death of Papinian	57
	His tyranny extended over the whole empire. Relaxation of discipline.	
217	Murder of Caracalla	58
	Imitation of Alexander. Election and character of Macrinus. Discontent of the senate. Discontent of the army. Macrinus attempts a reformation of the army	59
	Death of the empress Julia. Education, pretensions and revolt of Elagabalus, called at first Bassianus	
218	and Antoninus. Defeat and death of Macri us. Elagabalus writes to the senate	60
219	Picture of Elagabalus. His superstition. His profligate and effeminate luxury	61
	Contempt of decency, which distinguished the Roman tyrants. Discontents of the army. Alexander	
221	Severus declared Cæsar. Sedition	
222	of the guards, and murder of Elagabalus. Accession of Alexander Severus. Power of his mother Mamæa	62
	His wise and moderate administration. Education and virtuous temper of Alexander. Journal of the life	
222—235	ordinary life. General happiness of the Roman world	63
	Alexander refuses the name of Antoninus. He attempts to reform the army. Seditions of the prætorian guards, and murder of Ulpian. Danger of Dion Cassius. Tumults of the legions	64
	Firmness of the emperor. Defects of his reign and character. Digression on the finances of the empire. Establishment of the tribute on Roman citizens	65
	Abolition of the tribute. Tributes of the provinces. Of Asia, Egypt, and Gaul. Of Africa and Spain. Of the isle of Gyarus. Amount of the revenue. Taxes on Roman citizens instituted by Augustus	66
	I. The customs. II. The excise. III. Tax on legacies and inheritances. Suited to the laws and manners	67
	Regulations of the emperors. Edict of Caracalla. The freedom of the city given to all the provincials for the purpose of taxation. Temporary reduction of the tribute. Consequences of the universal freedom of Rome	68

CHAPTER VII.

The elevation and tyranny of Maximin.—Rebellion in Africa and Italy, under the authority of the senate.—Civil wars and seditions.—Violent deaths of Maximin and his son, of Maximus and Balbinus, and of the three Gordians. —Usurpation and secular games of Philip.

	The apparent ridicule and solid advantages of hereditary succession. Want of it in the Roman empire productive of the greatest calamities. Birth and fortunes of Maximin. His	
235	military service and honour. Conspiracy of Maximin	68

A. D. **Page**

Murder of Alexander Severus. Tyranny of Maximin. Oppression of
the provinces 70
237 Revolt in Africa. Character and elevation of the two Gordians. They
solicit the confirmation of their authority. The senate ratifies the
election of the Gordians 71
Declares Maximin a public enemy.
Assumes the command of Rome and
Italy. Prepares for a civil war.
237 Defeat and death of the two Gordians. Election of Maximus and
Balbinus by the senate 72
Their characters. Tumult at Rome.
The younger Gordian is declared
Cæsar. Maximin prepares to attack
the senate, and their emperors 73
238 Marches into Italy. Siege of Aqui-
238 leia. Conduct of Maximus. Murder
of Maximin and his son. His por-
trait. Joy of the Roman world 74
238 Sedition at Rome. Discontent of the
prætorian guards. Massacre of
Maximus and Balbinus. The third
Gordian remains sole emperor 75
Innocence and virtues of Gordian.
240, 242 Administration of Misitheus. The
243 Persian war. The arts of Philip.
244 Murder of Gordian. Form of a military republic 76
248 Reign of Philip. Secular games. Decline of the Roman empire 77

CHAPTER VIII.

*Of the state of Persia after the restoration of the
monarchy by Artaxerxes.*

The barbarians of the east and of the
north. Revolutions of Asia 77
The Persian monarchy restored by Artaxerxes. Reformation of the Ma-
gian religion 78
Persian theology, two principles. Religious worship 79
Ceremonies and moral precepts. En-
couragement of agriculture. Power
of the Magi. Spirit of persecution 80
Establishment of the royal authority
in the provinces. Extent and population of Persia. Recapitulation of
the war between the Parthian and
165 Roman empires. Cities of Seleucia
and Ctesiphon 81
216 Conquest of Osrhoene by the Romans.
230 Artaxerxes claims the provinces of
Asia, and declares war against the
233 Romans. Pretended victory of Alexander Severus 82
240 More probable account of the war.
Character and maxims of Artaxerxes. Military power of the Persians.
Their infantry contemptible. Their
cavalry excellent 83

CHAPTER IX.

*The state of Germany till the invasion of the
barbarians, in the time of the emperor Decius.*

Extent of Germany 84
Climate. Its effects on the natives.
Origin of the Germans 85
Fables and conjectures. The Germans
ignorant of letters—of arts and agriculture—of the use of metals 86
Their indolence. Their taste for strong
liquors. State of population 87
German freedom. Assemblies of the
people. Authority of the princes
and magistrates. More absolute
over the property, than over the
persons, of the Germans 88
Voluntary engagements. German
chastity. Its probable causes 89
Religion. Its effects in peace. Its effects in war. The bards. Causes
which checked the progress of the
Germans 90
Want of arms. Want of discipline.
Civil dissensions of Germany. Fo-
mented by the policy of Rome 91
Transient union against Marcus Antoninus. Distinction of the German
tribes. Numbers 92

CHAPTER X.

*The emperors Decius, Gallus, Æmilianus, Va-
lerian, and Gallienus.—The general irruption
of the barbarians.—The thirty tyrants.*

248—268 The nature of the subject. The
249 emperor Philip. Services, revolt,
victory, and reign of the emperor
Decius 92
250 He marches against the Goths. Origin of the Goths from Scandinavia.
Religion of the Goths. Institutions
and death of Odin 93
Agreeable but uncertain hypothesis
concerning Odin. Emigration of the
Goths from Scandinavia into Prussia. Emigration from Prussia to the
Ukraine. The Gothic nation increa-
ses in its march 94
Distinction of the Germans and Sarmatians. Description of the Ukraine. The Goths invade the Ro-
250 man provinces. Various events of
the Gothic war 95
251 Decius revives the office of censor in
the person of Valerian. The design
impracticable, and without effect.
Defeat and death of Decius and his
son 96
251, 252 Election of Gallus. Retreat of
the Goths. Gallus purchases peace
by the payment of an annual tribute.
253 Popular discontent. Victory and
revolt of Æmilianus. Gallus aban-

A. D. **Page**

doned and slain. Valerian reven-
ges the death of Gallus, and is acknowledged emperor 97
253—268 Character of Valerian. General
misfortunes of the reigns of Valerian
and Gallienus. Inroads of the barbarians. Origin and confederacy of the
Franks. They invade Gaul 98
They ravage Spain, and pass over into Africa. Origin and renown of the
Suevi. A mixed body of Suevi assume the name of Alemanni. Invade
Gaul and Italy. Are repulsed from
Rome by the senate and people. The
senators excluded by Gallienus from
the military service 99
Gallienus contracts an alliance with
the Alemanni. Inroads of the Goths.
Conquest of the Bosphorus by the
Goths. The Goths acquire a naval
force. First naval expedition of the
Goths. The Goths besiege and take
Trebizond 100
The second expedition of the Goths.
They plunder the cities of Bithynia.
Retreat of the Goths. Third naval
expedition of the Goths. They pass
the Bosphorus and the Hellespont 101
Ravage Greece, and threaten Italy.
Their divisions and retreat. Ruin
of the temple of Ephesus. Conduct
of the Goths at Athens 102
260 Conquest of Armenia by the Persians.
Valerian marches into the east. Is
defeated and taken prisoner by Sapor
king of Persia. Sapor overruns Syria, Cilicia, and Cappadocia. Boldness and success of Odenathus
against Sapor 103
Treatment of Valerian. Character and
administration of Gallienus. The
thirty tyrants. Their real number
was no more than nineteen 104
Character and merit of the tyrants.
Their obscure birth. The causes of
their rebellion. Their violent deaths.
Fatal consequences of these usurpa-
tions 105
Disorders of Sicily. Tumults of Alexandria. Rebellion of the Isaurians.
Famine and pestilence 106
Diminution of the human species 107

CHAPTER XI.

*Reign of Claudius.—Defeat of the Goths.—Vic-
tories, triumph, and defeat of Aurelian.*

268 Aureolus invades Italy, is defeated
and besieged at Milan. Death of
Gallienus. Character and elevation
of the emperor Claudius 107
268 Death of Aureolus. Clemency and
269 justice of Claudius. He undertakes
the reformation of the army. The
Goths invade the empire 108
270 Distress and firmness of Claudius.
His victory over the Goths. Death
of the emperor, who recommends
Aurelian for his successor. The attempt and fall of Quintilius 109
Origin and services of Aurelian. Aurelian's successful reign. His severe
discipline. He concludes a treaty
with the Goths, he resigns to them
the province of Dacia 110
270 The Alemannic war. The Alemanni
invade Italy. They are at last van-
quished by Aurelian 111
271 Superstitious ceremonies. Fortifications of Rome. Aurelian suppresses
the two usurpers. Succession of
usurpers in Gaul. The reign and defeat of Tetricus 112
272 Character of Zenobia. Her beauty
and learning. Her valour. She re-
venges her husband's death. She
reigns over the east and Egypt 113
272 The expedition of Aurelian. The
emperor defeats the Palmyrenians
in the battles of Antioch and Emesa.
The state of Palmyra. It is besieged
by Aurelian 114
273 Aurelian becomes master of Zenobia
and of the city. Behaviour of Zenobia. Rebellion and ruin of Palmyra.
Aurelian suppresses the rebellion of
274 Firmus in Egypt. Triumph of Aurelian 115
His treatment of Tetricus and Zenobia. His magnificence and devotion.
He suppresses a sedition at Rome.
Observations upon it 116
275 Cruelty of Aurelian. He marches into the east and is assassinated 117

CHAPTER XII.

*Conduct of the army and senate after the death of
Aurelian.—Reigns of Tacitus, Probus, Carus,
and his sons.*

Extraordinary contest between the
army and the senate for the choice
of an emperor 117
275 A peaceful interregnum of eight
months. The consul assembles the
senate. Character of Tacitus 118
He is elected emperor. He accepts
the purple. Authority of the senate.
276 Their joy and confidence. Tacitus
is acknowledged by the army. The
Alani invade Asia, and are repulsed
by Tacitus 119
276 Death of the emperor Tacitus. Usurpation and death of his brother Flo-
rianus. Their family subsists in ob-
scurity. Character and elevation of
the emperor Probus. His respectful
conduct towards the senate 120
277 Victories of Probus over the barbarians. He delivers Gaul from the invasion of the Germans 121

A. D. **Page**

He carries his arms into Germany. He
builds a wall from the Rhine to the
Danube. Introduction and settlement of the barbarians 122
279 Daring enterprise of the Franks. Re-
280 volt of Saturninus in the east.—Of
281 Bonosus and Proculus in Gaul. Triumph of the emperor Probus. His
discipline 123
282 His death. Election and character of
Carus. The sentiments of the senate
and people. Carus defeats the Sarmatians, and marches into the east 124
283 He gives audience to the Persian am-
283 bassadors. His victories and extraordinary death. He is succeeded by
his two sons, Carinus and Nume-
284 rian. Vices of Carinus 125
He celebrates the Roman games.
Spectacles of Rome. The amphi-
theatre 126
Return of Numerian with the army
from Persia. Death of Numerian. 127
284 Election of the emperor Diocletian 128
285 Defeat and death of Carinus 128

CHAPTER XIII.

*The reign of Diocletian and his three associates,
Maximian, Galerius, and Constantius.—Gen-
eral re-establishment of order and tranquillity.
—The Persian war, victory, and triumph.—
The new form of administration.—Abdication
and retirement of Diocletian and Maximian.*

285 Elevation and character of Diocletian.
His clemency and victory 128
286 Association and character of Maxi-
292 mian. Association of two Cæsars,
Galerius and Constantius. Depart-
ments and harmony of the four prin-
287 ces. Series of events. State of the
peasants of Gaul 129
287 Their rebellion and chastisement. Revolt of Carausius in Britain. Im-
289 portance of Britain. Power of Carausius 130
289 Acknowledged by the other emperors.
294 His death. Recovery of Britain by
Constantius. Defence of the fron-
tiers. Fortifications. Dissensions of
the barbarians. Conduct of the emperors 131
Valour of the Cæsars. Treatment of
the barbarians. Wars of Africa and
296 Egypt. Conduct of Diocletian in
Egypt 132
He suppresses books of alchymy. No-
velty and progress of that art. The
282 Persian war. Tiridates the Arme-
286 nian. His restoration to the throne
of Armenia. State of the country.
Revolt of the people and nobles.
Story of Mamgo 133
296 The Persians recover Armenia. War
between the Persians and the Romans. Defeat of Galerius. His re-
297 ception by Diocletian. Second campaign of Galerius 134
His victory. His behaviour to his royal captives. Negociation for peace.
Speech of the Persian ambassador.
Answer of Galerius. Moderation
of Diocletian. Conclusion of a treaty of peace 135
Articles of the treaty. The Aboras
fixed as the limits between the empires. Cession of five provinces beyond the Tigris. Armenia. Iberia.
303 Triumph of Diocletian and Maximian 136
Long absence of the emperors from
Rome. Their residence at Milan.
At Nicomedia. Debasement of
Rome and of the senate. New bodies of guards, Jovians and Hercu-
leans 137
Civil magistracies laid aside. Imperial dignity and titles. Diocletian
assumes the diadem, and introduces
the Persian ceremonial 138
New form of administration, two Au-
gusti, and two Cæsars. Increase
of taxes. Abdication of Diocletian
and Maximian. Resemblance to
304 Charles the fifth. Long illness of
Diocletian 139
His prudence. Compliance of Maximian. Retirement of Diocletian at
313 Salona. His philosophy. His death.
Description of Salona and the adja-
cent country 140
Of Diocletian's palace. Decline of
the arts—of letters. The new Plato-
nists 141

CHAPTER XIV.

*Troubles after the abdication of Diocletian.—
Death of Constantius.—Elevation of Constantine and Maxentius.—Six emperors at the same
time.—Death of Maximian and Galerius.—
Victories of Constantine over Maxentius and
Licinius.—Reunion of the empire under the authority of Constantine.*

305—323 Period of civil wars and confu-
sion. Character and situation of
Constantius—of Galerius. The two
Cæsars, Severus and Maximin 142
Ambition of Galerius disappointed by
274 two revolutions. Birth, education,
306 and escape of Constantine. Death of
Constantius, and elevation of Constantine 143
He is acknowledged by Galerius, who
gives him only the title of Cæsar, and
that of Augustus to Severus. The
others and sisters of Constantine.
Discontent of the Romans at the ap-
prehension of taxes 144
306 Maxentius declared emperor of Rome.
Maximian re-assumes the purple.

CONTENTS.

A. D.   Page
307 Defeat and death of Severus. Maximin gives his daughter Fausta, and the title of Augustus, to Constantine. Galerius invades Italy, 145
307 His retreat. Elevation of Licinius to
308 the rank of Augustus. Elevation of Maximin. Six emperors. Misfortunes of Maximin 146
310, 311 His death. Death of Galerius. His dominion shared between Maximin and Licinius 147
306—312 Administration of Constantine in Gaul. Tyranny of Maxentius in Italy and Africa. Civil war between
312 Constantine and Maxentius 148
Preparations. Constantine passes the Alps. Battle of Turin 149
Siege and battle of Verona. Indolence and fears of Maxentius 150
312 Victory of Constantine near Rome. 151
His reception. His conduct at Rome
313 His alliance with Licinius. War between Maximin and Licinius. The defeat of Maximin. His death. Cruelty of Licinius. Unfortunate fate of the empress Valeria and her mother 152
314 Quarrel between Constantine and Li-
314 cinius. First civil war between them 153
Battle of Cibalis. Battle of Mardia.
315—323 Treaty of peace. General peace and laws of Constantine 154
322, 323 The Gothic war 155
Second civil war between Constantine and Licinius. Battle of Hadrianople. Siege of Byzantium, and naval victory of Crispus 156
323 Battle of Chrysopolis. Submission and
324 death of Licinius. Re-union of the empire 157

CHAPTER XV.

The progress of the christian religion, and the sentiments, manners, numbers, and condition of the primitive christians.

Importance of the inquiry. Its difficulties 157
Five causes of the growth of christianity. I. THE FIRST CAUSE. Zeal of the Jews 158
Its gradual increase. Their religion better suited to defence than conquest 159
More liberal zeal of christianity. Obstinacy and reasons of the believing Jews. The Nazarine church of Jerusalem 160
The Ebionites. The Gnostics 161
Their sects, progress, and influence. The dæmons considered as the gods of antiquity 162
Abhorrence of the christians for idolatry. Ceremonies. Arts. Festivals. Zeal for christianity 163
II. THE SECOND CAUSE. The doctrine of the immortality of the soul among the philosophers. Among the pagans of Greece and Rome. Among the barbarians and the Jews 164
Among the christians. Approaching end of the world. Doctrine of the millennium 165
Conflagration of Rome and of the world. The pagans devoted to eternal punishment 166
Were often converted by their fears. III. THE THIRD CAUSE. Miraculous powers of the primitive church. Their truth contested. Our perplexity in defining the miraculous period 167
Use of the primitive miracles. IV. THE FOURTH CAUSE. Virtues of the first christians. Effects of their repentance. Care of their reputation 168
Morality of the fathers. Principles of human nature. The primitive christians condemn pleasure and luxury 169
Their sentiments concerning marriage and chastity. Their aversion to the business of war and government 170
V. THE FIFTH CAUSE. The christians active in the government of the church. Its primitive freedom and equality. Institutions of bishops as presidents of the college of presbyters 171
Provincial councils. Union of the church. Progress of episcopal authority 172
Pre-eminence of the metropolitan churches. Ambition of the Roman pontiff. Laity and clergy. Oblations and revenue of the church 173
Distribution of the revenue 174
Excommunication. Public penance. The dignity of episcopal government 175
Recapitulation of the five causes. Weakness of polytheism. The scepticism of the pagan world proved favourable to the new religion. And to the peace and union of the Roman empire 176
Historical view of the progress of christianity. In the east. The church of Antioch. In Egypt 177
In Rome. In Africa and the western provinces 178
Beyond the limits of the Roman empire. General proportion of christians and pagans. Whether the first christians were mean and ignorant. Some exceptions with regard to learning 179
To rank and fortune. Christianity most favourably received by the poor and simple. Rejected by some eminent men of the first and second centuries. Their neglect of prophecy 180

A. D.   Page
Of miracles. General silence concerning the darkness of the passion 181

CHAPTER XVI.

The conduct of the Roman government towards the christians, from the reign of Nero to that of Constantine.

Christianity persecuted by the Roman emperors 181
Inquiry into their motives. Rebellious spirit of the Jews. Toleration of the Jewish religion. The Jews were a people which followed, the christians a sect which deserted, the religion of their fathers 182
Christianity accused of atheism, and mistaken by the people and philosophers. The union and assemblies of the christians considered as a dangerous conspiracy 183
Their manners calumniated. Their imprudent defence 184
Idea of the conduct of the emperors towards the christians. They neglected the christians as a sect of Jews. The fire of Rome under the reign of Nero 185
Cruel punishment of the christians as the incendiaries of the city. Remarks on the passage of Tacitus relative to the persecution of the christians by Nero. 186
Oppression of the Jews and christians by Domitian 187
Execution of Clemens the consul. Ignorance of Pliny concerning the christians. Trajan and his successors establish a legal mode of proceeding against them 188
Popular clamours. Trials of the christians 189
Humanity of the Roman magistrates. Inconsiderable number of martyrs 190
257 Example of Cyprian, bishop of Carthage. His danger and flight. His banishment. His condemnation 191
His martyrdom. Various incitements to martyrdom. Ardour of the first christians 192
Gradual relaxation. Three methods of escaping martyrdom 193
Alternatives of severity and toleration. The ten persecutions. Supposed edicts of Tiberius and Marcus Antoninus. State of the christians in the reigns of Commodus and Severus 194
211—249 Of the successors of Severus. 195
244 Of Maximin, Philip, and Decius
253—260 Of Valerian, Gallienus, and his successors. Paul of Samosata.
270 manners. He is degraded from the see of Antioch 196
The sentence is executed by Aurelian.
284—303 Peace and prosperity of the church under Diocletian. Progress of zeal and superstition among the pagans 197
Maximian and Galerius punish a few christian soldiers. Galerius prevails on Diocletian to begin a general persecution 198
303 Demolition of the church of Nicomedia. The first edict against the christians. Zeal and punishment of a christian 199
Fire of the palace of Nicomedia imputed to the christians. Execution of the first edict. Demolition of the churches 200
303—311 Subsequent edicts. General idea of the persecution. In the western provinces, under Constantius and Constantine. In Italy and Africa, under Maximian and Severus 201
And under Maxentius. In Illyricum and the east, under Galerius and
311 Maximin. Galerius publishes an edict of toleration 202
Peace of the church. Maximin pre-
313 pares to renew the persecution. End of the persecutions. Probable account of the sufferings of the martyrs and confessors 203
Number of martyrs 204
Conclusion 205

CHAPTER XVII.

Foundation of Constantinople.—Political system of Constantine, and his successors.—Military Discipline.—The palace.—The finances.

324 Design of a new capital 205
Situation of Byzantium. Description of CONSTANTINOPLE. The Bosphorus 206
The port of Constantinople. The Propontis. The Hellespont 207
Advantages of Constantinople. Foundation of the city. Its extent 208
Progress of the work. Edifices 209
330 or 334 Population. Privileges 210
300—500 Dedication. Form of government in the Roman empire. Hierarchy of the state 211
Three ranks of honour. Four divisions of office. I. The consuls 212
The patricians. II. The prætorian præfects 213
The præfects of Rome and Constantinople 214
The proconsuls, vice-præfects, &c. 215
The governors of the provinces
The profession of the law. III. The military officers 216
Distinction of the troops. Reduction of the legions 217
Difficulty of levies. Increase of barbarian auxiliaries. IV. Seven ministers of the palace 218
1. The chamberlain. 2. The master

A. D.   Page
of the offices. 3. The quæstor. 4. The public treasurer 219
5. The private treasurer. 6, 7. The counts of the domestics. Agents, or official spies. Use of torture 220
Finances. The general tribute, or indiction 221
Assessed in the form of a capitation 222
Capitation on trade and industry 223
Free gifts. Conclusion 224

CHAPTER XVIII.

Character of Constantine.—Gothic war.—Death of Constantine.—Division of the empire among his three sons.—Persian war.—Tragic death of Constantine the younger, and Constans.—Usurpation of Magnentius.—Civil war.—Victory of Constantius.

Character of Constantine 224
His virtues. His vices. His family 225
324 Virtues of Crispus. Jealousy of Con-
325 stantine. Edict of Constantine.
326 Disgrace and death of Crispus 226
The empress Fausta 227
The sons and nephews of Constantine. Their education. Manners of the Sarmatians 228
Their settlement near the Danube.
331 The Gothic war 229
334 Expulsion of the Sarmatians. Death
337 and funeral of Constantine. Factions of the court 230
337 Massacre of the princes. Division
310 of the empire. Sapor, king of Persia 231
State of Mesopotamia and Armenia.
342, 337—360 Death of Tiridates. The Persian war. Battle of Singara 232
338, 346, 350 Siege of Nisibis 233
340 Civil war, and death of Constantine.
350 Murder of Constans. Magnentius and Vetranio assume the purple 234
Constantius refuses to treat. Deposes Vetranio 235
351 Makes war against Magnentius. Battle of Mursa 336
352, 353 Conquest of Italy. Last defeat and death of Magnentius 237

CHAPTER XIX.

Constantius sole emperor.—Elevation and death of Gallus.—Danger and elevation of Julian.—Sarmatian and Persian wars.—Victories of Julian in Gaul.

351 Power of the eunuchs. Education of Gallus and Julian 238
Gallus declared Cæsar. Cruelty and
354 imprudence of Gallus. Massacre of the imperial ministers 239
Dangerous situation of Gallus. His disgrace and death. The danger and escape of Julian 240
355 He is sent to Athens. Recalled to Milan 241
Declared Cæsar. Fatal end of Sylva-
357 nus. Constantius visits Rome 242
357, 358, 359 A new obelisk. The Quadian and Sarmatian war 243
358 The Persian negociation 244
359 Invasion of Mesopotamia by Sapor. Siege of Amida 245
360 Siege of Singara. Conduct of the Romans. Invasion of Gaul by the Germans 246
356 Conduct of Julian. His first campaign in Gaul 247
357 His second campaign. Battle of Strasburg 248
358 Julian subdues the Franks. Makes
357, 358, 359 three expeditions beyond the Rhine 249
Restores the cities of Gaul 250
Civil administration of Julian. Description of Paris 251

CHAPTER XX.

The motives, progress, and effects of the conversion of Constantine.—Legal establishment of the christian or catholic church.

306—337 Date of the conversion of Constantine 251
306—312 His pagan superstition. He pro-
313 tects the christians of Gaul. Edict of Milan 252
Use and beauty of the christian morality. Theory and practice of passive obedience 253
324 Divine right of Constantine. General edict of toleration. Loyalty and zeal of the christian party 254
Expectation and belief of a miracle. I. The *Labarum*, or standard of the cross. II. The dream of Constantine 255
III. Appearance of a cross in the sky. The conversion of Constantine might be sincere 256
The fourth eclogue of Virgil. Devotion and privileges of Constantine. Delay of his baptism till the approach of death. Propagation of christianity 258
312—438 Change of the national religion. Distinction of the spiritual and temporal powers 259
State of the bishops under the christian emperors. I. Election of bishops 260
II. Ordination of the clergy. III. Property 261
IV. Civil jurisdiction 262
V. Spiritual censures. VI. Freedom of public preaching 263
VII. Privilege of legislative assemblies 264

A. D.

CHAPTER XXI.

Page

*Persecution of heresy.—The schism of the Dona-
tists.—The Arian controversy.—Athanasius.—
Distracted state of the church and empire under Constantine and his sons.—Toleration of
paganism.*

312 African controversy. Schism of the
315 Donatists   265
A. C.
360. The Trinitarian controversy. The
system of Plato. The Logos   266
300 Taught in the school of Alexandria   267
A. D.
97 Revealed by the apostle St. John   267
The Ebionites and Docetes   268
Mysterious nature of the Trinity.
Zeal of the christians. Authority of
the church   269
318 Factions. Heterodox opinions of Arius.
Three systems of the Trinity. I.
Arianism. II. Tritheism   270
325 III. Sabellianism. Council of Nice.
The Homoousion Arian creeds   271
Arian sects   272
Faith of the western, or Latin, church.
360 Council of Rimini. Conduct of the
emperors in the Arian controversy.
324 Indifference of Constantine   273
325, 328—337 His zeal. He persecutes the
Arian and the orthodox party. Con-
337—361 stantius favours the Arians
Arian councils. Character and ad-
ventures of Athanasius   274
330 Persecution against Athanasius   275
336, 341 His first exile. His second ex-   276
ile   277
349, 351 His restoration. Resentment of
353—355 Constantius. Councils of Arles
and Milan   278
355 Condemnation of Athanasius. Exiles   279
356 Third expulsion of Athanasius from
Alexandria. His behaviour   280
356—362 His retreat. Arian bishops   281
Divisions. I. Rome. II. Constanti-
nople   282
345, &c. Cruelty of the Arians. The revolt
and fury of the Donatist Circumcel-
lions   283
312—361 Their religious suicides. General
character of the christian sects   284
Toleration of paganism by Constan-
tine. By his sons   285

CHAPTER XXII.

*Julian is declared emperor by the legions of
Gaul.—His march and success.—The death of
Constantius.—Civil administration of Julian.*

The jealousy of Constantius against
Julian   286
360 Fears and envy of Constantius. The
legions of Gaul are ordered to march
into the east. Their discontents   287
They proclaim Julian emperor. His
protestations of innocence   288
360, 361 His embassy to Constantius. His
fourth and fifth expeditions beyond
361 the Rhine. Fruitless treaty and de-
claration of war   289
Julian prepares to attack Constantius.
His march from the Rhine into Illy-
ricum   290
He justifies his cause   291
361 Hostile preparations. Death of Constantius   292
361 Julian enters Constantinople. Is acknowledged by the whole empire.
His civil government and private
life   293
Reformation of the palace. Chamber
of justice   294
Punishment of the innocent and the
guilty. Clemency of Julian   295
His love of freedom and the republic.
His care of the Grecian cities. Ju-
lian an orator and a judge   296
His character   297

CHAPTER XXIII.

*The religion of Julian.—Universal toleration.—
He attempts to restore and reform the pagan
worship—to rebuild the temple of Jerusalem.—
His artful persecution of the christians.—Mutual zeal and injustice.*

351 Religion of Julian   297
His education and apostasy. He em-
braces the mythology of paganism.   298
The allegories. Theological system
of Julian   299
Fanaticism of the philosophers. Initi-
ation and fanaticism of Julian. His
religious dissimulation   300
361 He writes against christianity. Universal toleration   301
361—363 Zeal and devotion of Julian in
the restoration of paganism. Refor-
mation of paganism   302
The philosophers. Conversions   303
The Jews. Description of Jerusalem.
Pilgrimages   304
363 Julian attempts to rebuild the tem-
ple. The enterprise is defeated   305
Perhaps by a preternatural event.
Partiality of Julian   306
He prohibits the christians from
teaching schools. Disgrace and op-
pression of the christians   307
They are condemned to restore the
pagan temples. The temple and sa-
cred grove of Daphne   308
362 Neglect and profanation of Daphne.
Removal of the dead bodies, and conflagration of the temple. Julian
shuts the cathedral of Antioch.

A. D.

Page

George of Cappadocia oppresses
Alexandria and Egypt   309
361 He is massacred by the people. He is
worshipped as a saint and martyr.
362 Restoration of Athanasius   310
He is persecuted and expelled by Ju-
361—363 lian. Zeal and imprudence of
the christians   311

CHAPTER XXIV.

*Residence of Julian at Antioch.—His successful
expedition against the Persians.—Passage of
the Tigris.—The retreat and death of Julian.
—Election of Jovian.—He saves the Roman army by a disgraceful treaty.*

362 The Cæsars of Julian. He resolves to
march against the Persians   312
Julian proceeds from Constantinople
to Antioch. Licentious manners of
the people of Antioch. Their aversion to Julian. Scarcity of corn, and
public discontent   313
Julian composes a satire against Anti-
344—390 och. The sophist Libanius   314
363 March of Julian to the Euphrates.
His design of invading Persia. Dis-
affection of the king of Armenia   315
Military preparations. Julian enters
the Persian territories. His march
over the desert of Mesopotamia   316
363 His success. Description of Assyria   317
Invasion of Assyria. Siege of Peri-
sabor. Siege of Maogamalcha   318
Personal behaviour of Julian. He
transports his fleet from the Eupha-
tes to the Tigris   319
Passage of the Tigris and victory of
the Romans   320
Situation and obstinacy of Julian. He
burns his fleet   321
Marches against Sapor. Retreat and
distress of the Roman army   322
363 Julian is mortally wounded. Death of
Julian   323
Election of the emperor Jovian   324
Danger and difficulty of the retreat.
Negociation and treaty of peace   325
The weakness and disgrace of Jovian.
He continues his retreat to Nisibis.
Universal clamour against the treaty
of peace   326
Jovian evacuates Nisibis, and re-
stores the five provinces to the Per-
sians. Reflections on the death of
Julian   327
On his funeral   328

CHAPTER XXV.

*The government and death of Jovian.—Election
of Valentinian, who associates his brother Valens, and makes the final division of the eastern
and western empires.—Revolt of Procopius.—
Civil and ecclesiastical administration.—Germany—Britain.—Africa.—The east.—The Danube.—Death of Valentinian.—His two sons,
Gratian and Valentinian II. succeed to the
western empire.*

363 State of the church   328
Jovian proclaims universal toleration.
His progress from Antioch   329
364 Jovian, with his infant son, assumes
the name and ensigns of the consul-
364 ship. Death of Jovian. Vacancy of
364 the throne. Election and character
of Valentinian. He is acknowledg-
ed by the army   330
364 Associates his brother Valens. The fi-
nal division of the eastern and wes-
365 tern empires. Revolt of Procopius   331
366 His defeat and death   332
373 Severe inquisition into the crime of
magic at Rome and Antioch   333
364—375 The cruelty of Valentinian and
Valens. Their laws and govern-
ment   334
Valentinian maintains the religious
367—378 toleration. Valens professes Arianism, and persecutes the catholics   335
373 Death of Athanasius. Just idea of
the persecution of Valens   336
370 Valentinian restrains the avarice of
366—384 the clergy. Ambition and luxu-
ry of Damasus, bishop of Rome   337
364—375, 365 Foreign wars. I. GERMANY.
366 The Alemanni invade Gaul. Their
defeat   338
368 Valentinian passes, and fortifies, the
371 Rhine. The Burgundians   339
The Saxons   340
II. BRITAIN. The Scots and Picts.
343—366 Their invasion of Britain
367—370 Restoration of Britain by Theo-
366 dosius. III. AFRICA. Tyranny of Ro-
manus   341
372, 373 Revolt of Firmus. Theodosius
recovers Africa   342
376 He is executed at Carthage. State of
365—378 Africa. IV. THE EAST. The Per-
sian war   343
384 The treaty of peace. Adventures of
Para, king of Armenia   344
V. The DANUBE. Conquests of Her-
366 manric. The cause of the Gothic
war   345
367—369, 374 Hostilities and peace. War
of the Quadi and Sarmatians   346
375 The expedition of Valentinian.   347
His death. The emperors Gratian and
Valentinian II.   348

CHAPTER XXVI.

*Manners of the pastoral nations.—Progress of
the Huns, from China to Europe.—Flight of*

A. D.

Page

the Goths.—They pass the Danube.—Gothic
war.—Defeat and death of Valens.—Gratian
invests Theodosius with the eastern empire.—
His character and success.—Peace and settlement of the Goths.

365 Earthquakes   349
376 The Huns and Goths. The pastoral
manners of the Scythians, or Tar-
tars. Diet   350
Habitations. Exercises   351
Government. Situation and extent of
Scythia, or Tartary   352
Original seat of the Huns. Their con-
quests in Scythia   353
A. C.
201 Their wars with the Chinese. Decline
141—87 and fall of the Huns   354
A. D.
100 Their emigrations. The white Huns
of Sogdiana. The Huns of the Vol-
ga   355
375 Their conquest of the Alani. Their
victories over the Goths   356
376 The Goths implore the protection of
Valens   357
They are transported over the Danube
into the Roman empire. Their dis-
tress and discontent   358
Revolt of the Goths in Mæsia, and
their first victories. They penetrate
into Thrace   359
Operations of the Gothic war   360
377 Union of the Goths with the Huns,
Alani, &c. Victory of Gratian over
378 the Alemanni   361
Valens marches against the Goths.
Battle of Hadrianople   362
The defeat of the Romans. Death of
the emperor Valens. Funeral ora-
tion of Valens and his army. The
Goths besiege Hadrianople   363
378, 379 They ravage the Roman provin-
ces. Massacre of the Gothic youth
in Asia   364
379 The emperor Gratian invests Theodo-
sius with the empire of the east.
Birth and character of Theodosius   365
379—382 His prudent and successful con-
duct of the Gothic war   366
381 Divisions, defeat, and submission, of
the Goths. Death and funeral of
Athanaric   367
386 Invasion and defeat of the Gruthungi,
383—395 or Ostrogoths. Settlement of the
Goths in Thrace and Asia   368
Their hostile sentiments   369

CHAPTER XXVII

*Death of Gratian.—Ruin of Arianism.—St. Am-
brose.—First civil war against Maximus.—
Character, administration, and penance of
Theodosius.—Death of Valentinian II.—Second
civil war, against Eugenius.—Death of Theodosius.*

379—383 Character and conduct of the em-
peror Gratian   369
383 His defects. Discontent of the Roman
troops. Revolt of Maximus in Bri-
tain   370
383 Flight and death of Gratian. Treaty
383—387 of peace between Maximus and
Theodosius   371
Baptism and orthodox edicts of Theo-
340—380 dosius. Arianism of Constanti-
nople   372
378 Gregory Nazianzen accepts the mis-
380 sion of Constantinople. Ruin of Ari-
anism at Constantinople   373
381 In the east. The council of Constantinople   374
Retreat of Gregory Nazianzen. Edicts
380—394 of Theodosius against the here-
tics   375
385 Execution of Priscillian and his asso-
375—397 ciates. Ambrose, archbishop of
Milan   376
385 His successful opposition to the em-
press Justina   377
387 Maximus invades Italy   378
Flight of Valentinian. Theodosius
takes arms in the cause of Valenti-
388 nian. Defeat and death of Maxi-
mus   379
387 Virtues of Theodosius. Faults of Theodosius   380
The sedition of Antioch. Clemency of
Theodosius   381
390 Sedition and massacre of Thessaloni-
388 ca. Influence and conduct of Am-
brose   382
390, 388—391 Penance of Theodosius. Gen-
391 erosity of Theodosius. Character of
Valentinian   383
392—394 His death. Usurpation of Eu-
392 genius. Theodosius prepares for
war   384
394 His victory over Eugenius   385
395 Death of Theodosius. Corruption of
the times. The infantry lay aside
their armour   386

CHAPTER XXVIII.

*Final destruction of paganism.—Introduction of
the worship of saints, and relics, among the
christians.*

378—395 The destruction of the pagan religion. State of paganism at Rome   387
384 Petition of the senate for the altar of
388 Victory. Conversion of Rome   388
381 Destruction of the temples in the provinces   389
The temple of Serapis at Alexandria   389
389 Its final destruction   390
390 The pagan religion is prohibited   391

A. D. Page
390—420 Oppressed. Finally extinguished 392
The worship of the christian martyrs. General reflections 393
I. Fabulous martyrs and relics. II. Miracles. III. Revival of polytheism 394
IV. Introduction of pagan ceremonies 395

CHAPTER XXIX.

Final division of the Roman empire between the sons of Theodosius.—Reign of Arcadius and Honorius. — Administration of Rufinus and Stilicho.—Revolt and defeat of Gildo in Africa.

395 Division of the empire between Arcadius and Honorius 395
386—395 Character and administration of Rufinus 396
395 He oppresses the east. He is disappointed by the marriage of Arcadius 397
Character of Stilicho, the minister and general of the western empire. His
385—408 military command 398
395 The fall and death of Rufinus 399
396 Discord of the two empires. Revolt
386—398 of Gildo in Africa 400
397 He is condemned by the Roman senate.
398 The African war 401
398 Defeat and death of Gildo. Marriage
398 and character of Honorius 402

CHAPTER XXX.

Revolt of the Goths.—They plunder Greece.—Two great invasions of Italy by Alaric and Radagaisus.—They are repulsed by Stilicho.—The Germans overrun Gaul.—Usurpation of Constantine in the west.—Disgrace and death of Stilicho.

395, 396 Revolt of the Goths. Alaric marches into Greece 403
397 He is attacked by Stilicho 404
398 Escapes to Epirus. Alaric is declared master-general of the eastern Illyricum. Is proclaimed king of the Visigoths
400—403 sigoths. He invades Italy 405
403 Honorius flies from Milan. He is pursued and besieged by the Goths 406
403 Battle of Pollentia. Boldness and retreat of Alaric 407
404 The triumph of Honorius at Rome. The gladiators abolished 408
404 Honorius fixes his residence at Ravenna. The revolutions of Scythia
405 Emigration of the northern Germans.
406 Radagaisus invades Italy—besieges Florence 410
406 Threatens Rome. Defeat and destruction of his army by Stilicho. The remainder of the Germans invade Gaul 411
407 Desolation of Gaul 412
Revolt of the British army. Constantine is acknowledged in Britain and Gaul. He reduces Spain 413
404—408 Negociation of Alaric and Stilicho. Debates of the Roman senate 414
408 Intrigues of the palace. Disgrace and death of Stilicho 415
His memory persecuted. The poet Claudian among the train of Stilicho's dependents 416

CHAPTER XXXI.

Invasion of Italy by Alaric.—Manners of the Roman senate and people.—Rome is thrice besieged, and at length pillaged by the Goths.—Death of Alaric.—The Goths evacuate Italy.—Fall of Constantine.—Gaul and Spain are occupied by the barbarians. — Independence of Britain.

408 Weakness of the court of Ravenna. Alaric marches to Rome 417
Hannibal at the gates of Rome. Genealogy of the senators 418
The Anician family. Wealth of the Roman nobles 419
Their manners. Character of the Roman nobles, by Ammianus Marcellinus 420
State and character of the people of Rome 422
Public distribution of bread, bacon, oil, wine, &c. Use of the public baths. Games and spectacles 423
408 Populousness of Rome. First siege of Rome by the Goths 424
409 Famine. Plague. Superstition. Alaric accepts a ransom, and raises the siege 425
Fruitless negociations for peace. Change and succession of ministers 426
409 Second siege of Rome by the Goths 427
410 Attalus is created emperor by the Goths and Romans. He is degraded by Alaric. Third siege and sack of Rome by the Goths 428
Respect of the Goths for the christian religion. Pillage and fire of Rome 429
Captives and fugitives 430
Sack of Rome by the troops of Charles
410 V. Alaric evacuates Rome, and ravages Italy 431
408—412 Possession of Italy by the Goths.
410 Death of Alaric. Adolphus, king of
412 the Goths, concludes a peace with the empire, and marches into Gaul 432
414 His marriage with Placidia. The Gothic treasures 433

A. D. Page
410—417 Laws for the relief of Italy and
413 Rome. Revolt and defeat of Heraclian, Count of Africa. Revolutions of Gaul and Spain 434
Character and victories of the general
411 Constantius. Death of the usurper
411—416 Constantine. Fall of the usurpers, Jovinus, Sebastian, and Attalus 435
409 Invasion of Spain by the Suevi, Vandals, Alani, &c. 436
414 Adolphus, king of the Goths, marches
415 into Spain. His death. The Goths
415—418 conquer and restore Spain 437
Their establishment in Aquitain. The
420, &c. Burgundians. State of the barbarians in Gaul. Revolt of Britain and
409 rians in Gaul. Revolt of Britain and Armorica 438
409—449 State of Britain 439
418 Assembly of the seven provinces of Gaul 440

CHAPTER XXXII.

Arcadius emperor of the east.—Administration and disgrace of Eutropius.—Revolt of Gainas.—Persecution of St. John Chrysostom.—Theodosius II. emperor of the east.—His sister Pulcheria.—His wife Eudocia.—The Persian war, and division of Armenia.

395—1453 The empire of the east. Reign
395—408 of Arcadius 440
395—399 Administration and character of Eutropius. Its venality and injustice 441
Ruin of Abundantius. Destruction of
397 Timasius. A cruel and unjust law of treason 442
399 Rebellion of Tribigild 443
400 Fall of Eutropius. Conspiracy and fall of Gainas 444
398 Election and merit of St. John Chrysostom 445
398—403 His administration and defects.
403 Chrysostom is persecuted by the empress Eudocia. Popular tumults at Constantinople 446
404, 407 Exile of Chrysostom. His death. His relics transported to Constantinople. Death of Arcadius 447
408—415 His supposed testament. Administration of Anthemius. Cha-
414—453 racter and administration of Pulcheria 448
Education and character of Theodosius the Younger. Character and adventures of the empress Eu-
421—460 docia 449
422 The Persian war 450
431—440 Armenia divided between the Persians and the Romans 451

CHAPTER XXXIII.

Death of Honorius.—Valentinian III. emperor of the west.—Administration of his mother Placidia.—Ætius and Boniface.—Conquest of Africa by the Vandals.

423 Last years and death of Honorius.
423—425 Elevation and fall of the usurper
425—455 John. Valentinian III. emperor of the west 452
425—450 Administration of his mother Placidia. Her two generals, Ætius
427 and Boniface. Error and revolt of Boniface in Africa 453
428 He invites the Vandals. Genseric
429 king of the Vandals. He lands in Africa. Reviews his army. The Moors. The Donatists 454
430 Tardy repentance of Boniface. Desolation of Africa. Siege of Hippo 455
430, 431 Death of St. Augustin. Defeat
432 and retreat of Boniface. His death.
431—439 Progress of the Vandals in Africa 456
439 They surprise Carthage. African exiles and captives. Fable of the seven sleepers 457

CHAPTER XXXIV.

The character, conquests, and court of Attila, king of the Huns.—Death of Theodosius the younger.—Elevation of Marcian to the empire of the east.

376—433 The Huns 458
Their establishment in modern Hungary. Reign of Attila. His fig-
433—453 ure and character 459
He discovers the sword of Mars. Acquires the empire of Scythia and
430—440 Germany. The Huns invade Persia 460
441, &c. They attack the eastern empire. Ravage Europe, as far as Constantinople 461
The Scythian or Tartar wars. State of the captives 462
446 Treaty of peace between Attila and the eastern empire. Spirit of the Azimuntines 463
Embassies from Attila to Constantinople. The embassy of Maximin to
448 Attila 464
The royal village and palace 465
The behaviour of Attila to the Roman ambassadors. The royal feast 466
Conspiracy of the Romans against the life of Attila. He reprimands and
450 forgives the emperor. Theodosius the younger dies. Is succeeded by Marcian 467

A. D. Page
CHAPTER XXXV.

Invasion of Gaul by Attila.—He is repulsed by Ætius and the Visigoths.—Attila invades and evacuates Italy.—The deaths of Attila, Ætius, and Valentinian the third.

450 Attila threatens both empires, and
435—454 prepares to invade Gaul. Character and administration of Ætius 468
His connection with the Huns and
410—451 Alani. The Visigoths in Gaul under the reign of Theodoric 469
435—539 The Goths besiege Narbonne, &c.
420—451 The Franks in Gaul under the Merovingian kings 470
The adventures of the princess Hono-
451 ria. Attila invades Gaul and besieges Orleans 471
Alliance of the Romans and Visigoths 472
Attila retires to the plains of Champagne. Battle of Chalons 473
452 Retreat of Attila. Invasion of Italy by Attila 474
Foundation of the republic of Venice 475
Attila gives peace to the Romans 476
453, 454 The death of Attila. Destruction of his empire 477
Valentinian murders the patrician Ætius. Valentinian ravishes the
455 wife of Maximus. Death of Valentinian. Symptoms of the decay and ruin of the Roman government 478

CHAPTER XXXVI.

Sack of Rome by Genseric, king of the Vandals.—His naval depredations.—Succession of the last emperors of the west.—Maximus, Avitus, Majorian, Severus, Anthemius, Olybrius, Glycerius, Nepos, Augustulus.—Total extinction of the western empire.—Reign of Odoacer, the first barbarian king of Italy.

439—455 Naval power of the Vandals.
455 The character and reign of the emperor Maximus 479
455, 456 His death. Sack of Rome by the Vandals 480
450—466 The emperor Avitus. Character of Theodoric, king of the Visigoths 481
456 His expedition into Spain 482
456, 457 Avitus is deposed. Character and elevation of Majorian 483
His salutary laws. The edifices of Rome 484
457—461 His salutary laws. The edifices of Rome 484
457 Majorian prepares to invade Africa 485
461 The loss of his fleet. His death. Ricimer reigns under the name of
461—467 Severus. Revolt of Marcellinus in Dalmatia 486
461—467 Revolt of Ægidius in Gaul. Na-
462, &c. val war of the Vandals. Negociations with the eastern empire 487
457—474 Leo, emperor of the east. An-
467—472 themius, emperor of the west 488
468 The festival of the Lupercalia. Preparations against the Vandals of Africa 489
462—472 Failure of the expedition. Conquest of the Visigoths in Spain and Gaul 490
468 Trial of Arvandus 491
471 Discord of Anthemius and Ricimer.
472 Olybrius, emperor of the west 492
472 Sack of Rome, and death of Anthemius. Death of Ricimer—of Oly-
472—475 brius. Julius Nepos and Glyce-
475 rius emperors of the west. The patrician Orestes 493
476 His son Augustulus, the last emperor
476—490 of the west. Odoacer, king of Italy.
476 or 479 aly. Extinction of the western empire 494
Augustulus is banished to the Lucul-
476—490 lan villa. Decay of the Roman empire 495
Character and reign of Odoacer. Miserable state of Italy 496

CHAPTER XXXVII.

Origin, progress, and effects of the monastic life.—Conversion of the barbarians to christianity and Arianism.—Persecution of the Vandals in Africa.—Extinction of Arianism among the barbarians.

I. INSTITUTION OF THE MONASTIC
305 LIFE. Origin of the monks. Antony and the monks of Egypt 497
341 Propagation of the monastic life at
328, 360 Rome. Hilarion in Palestine. Ba-
370 sil in Pontus. Martin in Gaul. Causes of the rapid progress of the monastic life 498
Obedience of the monks. Their dress and habitations 499
Their diet. Their manual labour. Their riches 500
Their solitude. Their devotion and visions. The Cœnobites and Anachorets 501
395—451 Simeon Stylites. Miracles and worship of the monks. Superstition of the age. II. CONVERSION OF THE BARBARIANS 502
360, &c. Ulphilus, apostle of the Goths.
400, &c. The Goths, Vandals, Burgundians, &c. embrace christianity. Motives of their faith 503
Effects of their conversion. They are involved in the Arian heresy 504
General toleration. Arian persecu-
429—477 tion of the Vandals. Genseric.
477, 484, 496 Hunneric. Gundamund. Thra-
523, 530 simund. Hilderic. Gelimer. A general view of the persecution in Africa 505

A. D.   Page
      Catholic frauds. Miracles   507
500—700 The ruin of Arianism among the
577—584 barbarians. Revolt and martyr-
      dom of Hermenegild in Spain. Con-
586—589 version of Recared and the Visi-
      goths of Spain   508
600, &c. Conversion of the Lombards of
612—712 Italy. Persecution of the Jews
      in Spain. Conclusion   509

            CHAPTER XXXVIII.

*Reign and conversion of Clovis.—His victories
over the Alemanni, Burgundians, and Visigoths.—Establishment of the French monarchy
in Gaul.—Laws of the barbarians.—State of
the Romans.—The Visigoths of Spain.—Conquest of Britain by the Saxons.*

476—485 The revolution of Gaul. Euric,
481—511 king of the Visigoths. Clovis,
      king of the Franks   510
486, 496 His victory over Syagrius. De-
      feat and submission of the Aleman-
      ni   511
                                                512
496 Conversion of Clovis
497, &c. Submission of the Armoricans
499   and the Roman troops. The Bur-
500   gundian war. Victory of Clovis   513
532 Final conquest of Burgundy by the
507   Franks. The Gothic war   514
508 Victory of Clovis. Conquest of Aqui-
      tain by the Franks   515
510, 536 Consulship of Clovis. Final es-

A. D.   Page
      tablishment of the French monar-
      chy in Gaul. Political controversy   516
Laws of the barbarians. Pecuniary
      fines for homicide   517
Judgments of God. Judicial combats   518
Division of land by the barbarians.
      Domain and benefices of the Mero-
      vingians. Private usurpations   519
Personal servitude. Example of Au-
      vergne   520
Story of Attalus   521
Privileges of the Romans in Gaul.
      Anarchy of the Franks   522
The Visigoths of Spain. Legislative
      assemblies of Spain. Code of the
      Visigoths   523
449 Revolution of Britain. Descent of the
455—582 Saxons. Establishment of the
      Saxon heptarchy   524
State of the Britons. Their resis-
      tance. Their flight. The fame of
      Arthur   525
Desolation of Britain. Servitude of
      the Britons.   526
Manners of the Britons   527
Obscure or fabulous state of Britain.
      Fall of the Roman empire in the west   528

*General observations on the fall of the Roman
empire in the west.*   528

            CHAPTER XXXIX.

*Zeno and Anastasius, emperors of the east.—
Birth, education, and first exploits of Theodo-

A. D.   Page
ric the Ostrogoth.—His invasion and conquest
of Italy.—The Gothic kingdom of Italy.—State
of the west.—Military and civil government.—
The senator Boethius.—Last acts and death of
Theodoric.*

455—475 Birth and education of Theodo-
      ric   531
474—491, 491—518 The reign of Zeno. The
475—488 reign of Anastasius. Service and
      revolt of Theodoric   532
489 He undertakes the conquest of Italy.
      His march   533
489—490 The three defeats of Odoacer. His
493   capitulation and death. Reign of
493—526 Theodoric, king of Italy. Parti-
      tion of lands   534
Separation of the Goths and Italians.
      Foreign policy of Theodoric   535
509 His defensive wars. His naval arma-
      ments. Civil government of Italy
      according to the Roman laws   536
500 Prosperity of Rome. Visit of Theodo-
      ric   537
Flourishing state of Italy. Theodoric
      an Arian. His toleration of the ca-
      tholics   538
Vices of his government. He is pro-
      voked to persecute the catholics.
      Character, studies, and honours, of
      Boethius   539
His patriotism. He is accused of
524   treason. His imprisonment and
      death   540
524, 526 Death of Symmachus. Remorse
      and death of Theodoric   541

GUIZOT'S PREFACE.

[TRANSLATION.]

To reprint a valuable work—to rectify, in an extensive history, omissions and errors the more important, because, lost in an immense number of facts, they are eminently fitted to deceive, both the superficial who believe all they read, and the attentive, who have no opportunity for investigation; such have been the motives which have determined me to publish with added notes, this new edition of the Decline and Fall of the Roman Empire by EDWARD GIBBON.

This period of history has been the subject of study and toil to a multitude of writers, of learned men, and even of philosophers. The gradual decline of that most extraordinary power, which had over-run and oppressed the world; the fall of this greatest of empires, built upon the ruins of so many kingdoms, republics, and states, both barbarous and civilized, and forming in its turn by its dismemberment, a multitude of states, republics, and kingdoms; the annihilation of the religion of Greece and Rome; the origin and progress of two new religions, which have occupied between themselves the fairest countries of the earth; the old age of the ancient world, the spectacle of its expiring glory and degenerate morals; the infancy of the modern world, the description of its first advances and of the new impulse given to mind and character; such a subject must necessarily fix the attention and excite the interest of those men who cannot see with indifference, such memorable epochs, or in the beautiful expression of Corneille,

"Un grand destin commence, un grand destin s'acheve."

Thus, learning, eloquence, and the spirit of philosophy, have emulously engaged in bringing to light, and picturing the ruins of this vast edifice whose fall had been preceded, and was to be followed by so much greatness. Messrs. de Tillemont, Lebeau, Ameilhou, Pagi, Eckhel, and a great number of other writers, French and foreign, have examined all its parts, they have searched among the rubbish for facts, details and dates, and by the aid of erudition more or less extensive, and of criticism more or less enlightened, have in some manner collected and arranged anew the scattered materials. Their works are of unquestionable utility, and I have no wish to diminish their merit, but in digging among the ruins they have sometimes buried themselves; either because they have voluntarily limited the subject and the circle of their researches, or because the very nature of their minds confined them within certain bounds. They have, while occupied in search of facts, neglected the general outline of ideas, they have explored and brought to light the ruins without re-erecting the monument. We do not find in their works those general views, which enable us to embrace at a glance a great extent of country—a long series of ages; and which make us distinguish clearly amidst the darkness of the past, the progress of the human species, ever changing its form but not its nature, its habits and not its passions, always arriving at the same results by different means; those great views, in fine, which constitute the philosophy of History, and without which it is only a mass of facts, as inconclusive, as they are disconnected.

Montesquieu, on the other hand, in his "Considerations sur les causes de la grandeur et de la decadence des Romains," glancing on every side with the eye of genius, has brought forward a multitude of thoughts, always profound and almost always new, but sometimes inaccurate, and authorized less by the nature and connection of facts, than by those rapid and ingenious deductions to which a superior mind too easily surrenders itself, because it finds a vivid pleasure in manifesting its power in this species of creation. Happily, by a beautiful provision, the errors of genius are fertile in truths, it may wander for a moment from the path it has opened, but the way is open and others follow with

xiii

more safety and circumspection. Gibbon, less able, less profound, of a less exalted genius **than** Montesquieu, made himself master of a subject whose richness and extent the other had pointed out; he followed with care the long array and progressive chain of facts, some of which only Montesquieu had selected and recalled, rather to attach them to his own ideas, than to make the reader acquainted with their progress and mutual influence. The English historian, eminently gifted with that penetration which traces events to causes, and with that sagacity which separates from causes seemingly true, those which really are so; born in an age when distinguished men carefully scrutinized every part of the social machine, and endeavored to discover its action, utility, effects, and importance, placed by his pursuits and by the reach of his mind on an equality with the master spirits of his age, brought to his researches into the materiel of history or the facts themselves, the criticism of a judicious and learned man, and to his views of the moral of history, or the relations which connect events and associate their authors with them, that of an able philosopher. He knew that history if confined to an account of facts merely, excites no other interest than that which men feel in the actions of their fellow men, and that to be really useful and true, it ought to look upon the face of society, whose image it retraces under all the different points of view from which it can be considered, by the statesman, the warrior, the magistrate, the financier, and the philosopher; by all those indeed who are capacitated by their situation or their intelligence to understand its different springs of action.

This thought, no less just than great, seems to have had its influence in the composition of the Decline and Fall of the Roman Empire. It is not merely an account of the events which agitated the Roman world from the accession of Augustus to the taking of Constantinople by the Turks, but the author has constantly connected with the history of events an account of the state of finances, of opinions, of morals, of the military system, and of those internal and concealed causes of prosperity or calamity which strengthen society, or secretly threaten its well-being and existence. Gibbon, faithful to the known but neglected law, which compels us always to make facts the basis of general reflections, and to follow step by step their slow but necessary course, has thus composed a work, remarkable for the extent of its views, though not for great elevation of thought, and full of positive and interesting results, notwithstanding the scepticism of its author.

The success of this work, in an age which had produced a Montesquieu, and which at the time of its publication possessed a Hume, a Robertson, and a Voltaire, certainly proves its merit, and the continuance of this success to the present time is a farther confirmation of its worth. In England, France, Germany, and among all the enlightened nations of Europe Gibbon is always cited as authority; and even those who have discovered some inaccuracies in his book, or who disapprove of his sentiments, do not attempt to remove his errors or to combat his opinions, except with a cautious respect due to superior merit. I have had occasion in the course of my investigations to consult the writings of philosophers who have treated of the finances of the Roman empire, of learned men who have studied its chronology, of theologians versed in ecclesiastical history, of civilians who have studied with care Roman jurisprudence, of orientalists who have devoted themselves to Arabic literature, of modern historians who have examined the subject of the crusades and their influence—and every one of these writers has observed and pointed out in the History of the Decline and Fall of the Roman Empire instances of carelessness, of false or at least incomplete views, and sometimes even omissions which they could not but believe voluntary. They have corrected some faults, and have opposed with success some assertions, but more frequently they have employed the researches and thoughts of Gibbon, either to show wherein they differ from him, or to substantiate their own researches and deductions. I may perhaps be permitted here to mention a certain suspense and uncertainty which I have myself experienced in studying this work. I prefer to incur the hazard of speaking of myself than to omit an observation which may set forth both merits and defects. After the first rapid perusal, which permitted me only to feel interested in a narrative always animated notwithstanding its length, always clear notwithstanding the variety of objects it presents in review before the eye, I entered into a minute examination of the details of which it is composed, and the opinion I then formed was, I confess, singularly severe. I found in certain chapters errors which appeared to me sufficiently important and numerous to warrant the belief that the work in some parts had been written with extreme negligence; in others there appeared a general tinge of partiality and prejudice which gave to the narration of facts that want of truth and justice which the English happily designate by the word *misrepresentation*. Mutilated quotations, and the involuntary or designed omission of certain passages, rendered me suspicious of the author's integrity. The grossness of this violation of the first law of history was

increased to my mind by the prolonged attention with which I scrutinized each phrase, each note and reflection—and in consequence I passed upon the whole work much too rigorous a judgment. After this careful study of the history, I permitted some time to elapse before again reviewing it. Another attentive and continuous perusal of the whole work, of the notes of the author, and of those which I have thought it right to add to them, has showed me how much I have exaggerated the importance of the strictures which Gibbon merited. I have been struck with the same errors, with the same partiality on certain subjects, but I found that I had been far from rightly appreciating the vastness of his research, the variety of his information, the extent of his knowledge, and, more than all, that truly philosophical justice of his mind which judges of the past as it would of the present, without being darkened by those clouds with which time surrounds the dead; and which often prevent us from seeing, that under the toga and in the senate, men were the same that they are still in our modern dress, and in our own councils—and that events transpired eighteen centuries ago in the same manner as they do now. I perceived also that Gibbon, notwithstanding his failings, was truly an able historian, that his history with all its defects would always be a good work, and that his errors might be corrected, and his prejudices opposed, without ceasing to admit that few men have united in a manner so complete and well defined, the qualities essential to an historian.

I have then attempted in my notes only to correct facts which appeared to me false or misrepresented, and to supply those, the omission of which might become a source of error. I am far from believing that this work of correction is complete. I have been very guarded in applying it to the History of the Decline and Fall of the Roman Empire in all its extent. It would enlarge too much a work already most voluminous, and add innumerable notes to the many notes of the author; my first and principal design, was to review with care those chapters devoted by Gibbon to the history of the establishment of christianity, and to re-establish in all their exactness, and place in their true light the facts of which they are composed. It is in those chapters therefore that I have made the most additions, other chapters also, as that which treats of the religion of the ancient Persians, or that in which the author exhibits a view of the state of ancient Germany and of the migrations of the people, have appeared to me to need elucidation and rectifying. Their importance will furnish my excuse. In general my work has not extended much beyond the first five volumes of the new edition. Almost all which concerns christianity is found in these volumes; in them also is seen the transition from the ancient to the modern world, from the manners and the thoughts of Roman Europe to those of our Europe, an epoch the most interesting and important to make clear in the whole work. Besides, later times have been treated of with great care by many different writers, so that the notes I have added to the last volume are few and concise, too much so perhaps; nevertheless I can affirm that I have rigidly observed the rule to say nothing which did not seem to me necessary, and to say it as briefly as possible. Much has been written for and against Gibbon. From the time his work appeared comments were made upon it as if it had been an ancient manuscript, and they were truly those of critics. Theologians, more than all others, have complained of the manner in which he has treated ecclesiastical history; they have attacked the XV and XVI chapters sometimes with reason, often with bitterness, but almost always with arms inferior to those of their adversary, who certainly possessed more knowledge, more genius, more insight into his subject than his opponents, as far at least as their works have been within the reach of my examination. Dr. Watson, since bishop of Landaff, published " *A series of letters, or An apology for Christianity*," the moderation and merit of which are acknowledged by Gibbon himself. [1] Priestley wrote "*A letter to an incredulous philosopher containing a view of the evidences of revealed religion, with observations upon the first two volumes of Mr. Gibbon.*" Dr. White in a course of sermons, of which Dr. S. Badcock was, it is said, the real author, and of which Dr. White furnished only the materials, traced a comparative view of the christian and mahommedan religions (1st edition, 1784, 8vo,) in which he often opposed Gibbon, and of which Gibbon himself speaks with esteem, (see *memoirs of his life,* p. 167, vol. 1st of *miscellaneous works* and his *letters,* nos. 82, 83, &c.) These three are the adversaries most worthy of consideration who have attacked our historian. A multitude of other writers joined them, Sir David Dalrymple, Dr. Chelsam, chaplain to the bishop of Worcester, [2] Mr. Davis, member of Baliol college, Oxford, Mr. East Apthorpe, rector of St. Mary le Bone, London, [3] J. Beattie, Mr. J. Melner, Mr.

---

[1] D. R. Watson's Apology for Christianity in a series of letters to Edward Gibbon, 1776, in 8vo.

[2] J. Chelsam's D. D. remarks on the two last chapters of the first vol. of Mr. Gibbon's History, &c. Oxford, 2nd Edition, 1778, 8vo.

[3] East Apthorpe's letters on the prevalence of christianity before its civil establishment with observations on Mr. Gibbon's History, &c. 1778, 8vo.

Taylor, Mr. Travis, prebendary of Chester, and vicar of Eastham,[1] Dr. Whitaker, an anonymous writer, who took only the name of the *Anonymous Gentleman*, Mr. H. Kett,[2] &c. &c. arrayed themselves against the new historian. He replied to some of them in a pamphlet entitled " A defence of some passages in the XV and XVI chapters of the History of the Decline and Fall of the Roman Empire."[3] This defence, victorious in some points and weak in others, but excessively bitter, revealed the irritation which these attacks had excited in Gibbon. This irritation, perhaps, indicated, that he did not feel himself entirely irreproachable; nevertheless, he altered none of his opinions in the rest of the work, which proves, at least, his sincerity. Although I have made great effort, I have been able to procure but a small part of these works. Those of Dr. Chelsam, of Mr. Davis, of Mr. Travis, and of the anonymous writer, are the only works that I have been able to obtain. I have received from them some interesting thoughts; and when I have not been able to explain or to defend them by higher authorities, I have mentioned to whom I was indebted for them. Not only in England have comments been made upon Gibbon. F. A. G. Wenck, professor of law at Leipsic, a very estimable literary man, undertook a translation of it into German. The first volume appeared at Leipsic in 1779. He also added notes, full of erudition, no less extensive than accurate. I have derived from them great assistance. Unfortunately, M. Wenck did not continue his undertaking. The remaining volumes have been translated by M. Schreiter, professor at Leipsic, who has added but a few notes, and those very unimportant. M. Wenck announced in his preface, that he should publish particular dissertations on the XV and XVI chapters, the object of which would be to examine the account given by Gibbon of the propagation of christianity. He has been dead, now, two years. Not having been informed of his death, I wrote to his son, and requested a copy of them. His son wrote in answer, that he had not been able to find them among his father's papers.

There is another German translation of Gibbon, with which I am not acquainted. I have been told that it contains no new notes. Many German theologians, as M. Walterstern,[4] M. Luderwald,[5] &c. have opposed Gibbon, especially in treating of the propagation of christianity. I am acquainted with the titles of their works only. M. Hugo, professor of law at Gottingen, published, in 1789, a translation of the XLIV chapter, in which Gibbon treats of Roman jurisprudence, with critical notes, some of which I have borrowed, but these notes establish, in general, few facts, and are not always sufficiently supported with proof.

In French, I have read but one dissertation against Gibbon, inserted in the seventh volume of the *Spectateur Francais*. It appeared to me very ordinary, and contains rather reasoning than facts.

Such, at least according to my knowledge, are the principal works of which the History of the Decline and Fall of the Roman Empire has been the subject. Those which I have examined, have been far from satisfactory to me ; and after having derived from them the most that was interesting, I have myself written, upon the various parts which remained to be examined, a critical work of some extent. I believe I ought here to mention the principal sources whence I have derived information and facts. Besides the original authors of which Gibbon availed himself, and to which I have referred as much as was in my power—such as the history of Augustus, Dion Cassius, Ammienus Marcellinus, Eusebius, Lactantius, &c. &c., I have consulted some of the best writers who have treated of the same subjects much more carefully and extensively, inasmuch as they have devoted themselves especially to the study of them. Concerning the history of the primitive church, the writings of the learned Gardner, the *Abridgement of Ecclesiastical History* by Spittler, the *Ecclesiastical History* of Flenke, the *History of the Constitution of the Christian Church* by M. Plauck, and a Manuscript by the same author upon the *History of the Doctrines of Christianity, History of Heresies* by C. G. F. Walch, the *Introduction to the New Testament* of Michaelis, the *Commentary upon the New Testament* of M. Paulus, the *History of Philosophy* by M. Tennemann, and particular dissertations, have been my principal resources. For the account of the migrations of the people of the north, the *History of the North* by Schlœzer, the *Universal History* of Gatterer, the *Ancient History of the Teutonic Race* by Adelung, *Memoriæ Populorum* ex *Historiis Byzantinis erutæ* by M. Stritter, have furnished me information which I should vainly have sought for elsewhere. To

---

1 *Letters to Edward Gibbon,* 2d edition, London, 1785, 8vo.
2 *H. Kett's Sermons at Bampton's Lecture,* 1791, 8vo. *H. Kett's representation of the conduct and opinions of the primitive christians, with remarks on certain assertions of Mr. Gibbon and Mr. Priestly, in eight sermons.*
3 *A vindication of some passages in the XV and XVI chapters of the History of the Decline and Fall of the Roman Empire.* The 2d edition which I have used was printed in London 1779.
4 *Die ausbreitung des christenthums aus naturlichen ursachen von W. S. von Walterstern.* Hamburg, 1788, 8vo.
5 *Die ausbreitung der christlichen religion, von J. B. Luderwald.* Helmstaedt, 1788, in 8vo.